Terrain

Poems by Julia Lisella

WordTech Editions

For Carol —
one of my best
teachers!
Hugs,
Julia —
Salem, MA
2008

Published by WordTech Editions
P.O. Box 541106
Cincinnati, OH 45254-1106

ISBN: 9781933456751
LCCN: 2007930916

Poetry Editor: Kevin Walzer
Business Editor: Lori Jareo

Cover Painting: *The Red Fence* by Adele Travisano. Courtesy of CherryStone Gallery, Wellfleet, MA.

Author Photo: Otha Sonnie.

Visit us on the web at www.wordtechweb.com

Terrain

for Ed, Renata, and Carl

Acknowledgments

With grateful acknowledgment to the editors of the following publications in which some of these poems first appeared, sometimes in slightly different form:

Crab Orchard Review: "Miscarriage"
descant: "Lucky"
Literary Mama: "Old Body"
The Local: "The Promise"
Many Mountains Moving: "Rosebush"
Mystic River Review: "Why It Is Difficult"
Paterson Literary Review: "Afternoons with My Mother"
Pebble Lake Review: "Buildings After the Ice Age"
Pedestal Magazine: "Children"
Pleiades: "May 21, 1999: Tomorrow Would Be the Day
        of Your Birth"
Sidelines: "Bedrest"
Solo: "Considering the Universe"
Sou'wester: "Early Song"
VIA: Voices in Italian Americana: "Our July"
Violet: "Miró Sees the Devil"
West Branch: "At Six Months"

"Song of the Third Generation" appears in *Unsettling America: An Anthology of Contemporary Multicultural Poetry* (New York: Penguin Books, 1994).

"Recovery Room" appears in *DKA: The Doc Kountze Annual,* Vol. 2 (Medford, MA: Doc Kountze Annual Committee, 2003).

"Grace" appears in *e: 2003 Emily Dickinson Award Anthology* (Universities West Press, Vol. 8, 2005).

The following poems appear in the chapbook *Love Song Hiroshima* (Finishing Line Press, 2004): "The Promise," "Our July," "Song of the Third Generation," "Afternoon With My Mother."

Epigraph for "Children" from "Sonogram" by Charlotte Mandel, *Sight Lines* (NY: Midmarch Arts Press, 1998). Used by permission of the publisher.

"The Shield" is written in response to W.H. Auden's poem, "The Shield of Achilles." "Miró Sees the Devil" is dedicated to Ed Kleifgen; "Public Beach" is for Ann Keniston and Cammy Thomas; "Birthday" is for Renata Kleifgen; "Buildings After the Ice Age" is for Brad Clompus.

Grateful acknowledgment is also due to the MacDowell Colony, the Millay Colony, and the Dorset Colony for residencies that made the writing of many of these poems possible.

With thanks to a community of writers I'm blessed to work with: Brad Clompus, Ann Keniston, Theodora Stratis, Cammy Thomas, and Rosamond Zimmerman, for their care and company, and to Robert Clawson for his editorial acumen. Finally, *un baccio* to my first teachers, my parents, Jean and Jules Lisella.

Contents

I. Third Generation

Rosebush

See here where the earth swells,
where he knocked back the rosebush, punishment for its branches
        collapsing atop

the Saturn? See how we name our cars for planets? See how
        these cars don't
bring us closer to the sun? See how we can't fly yet? And see
        how the rosebush

sat in its aged roots, not as aged as the house it had leaned on
        for years,
but old enough to know it had come to its own starvation,
        flailing in the wind

on an angry night when my husband yelled to stop my anger,
        get the hell out, and I did
go grocery shopping and I did come back though I said I wouldn't

and that rosebush was just gone at his hands, but at its own self,
        too. Because
it couldn't stand up anymore. Attacking us each day with its
        useless thorns. Because

it couldn't protect what it did best. Each day I feel I am getting
        younger
in the awful way, not in the happy *Cosmo* way, but in the awful
        empathic way

born of remembering how hard it was to get to the age I am. See
        the moon
tonight? It is smaller now that we know there are many

galaxies, and planets

with their own moons out there, their own dried up rivers,
        their own ice ages and
fossilized lives. See how I cannot bear to bear witness to the
        loss of our lovely

unwieldy rosebush that extended its growth too far and too
        long and too dangerously
into the other world of our driveway? See how I must look up
        at the moon and down at

my shoes, and away from my car, away from my children, my
        husband, my unwritten
books? See how those gentle brown stumps of life that will
        come back better than before

can't convince me that it's alright right now to be in my little
        middle-class
heaven? See the mistakes we've made being less than the
        boys and the girls in us

dreamed of becoming? See how I've made my problem yours,
the groundswell swaying me down to the ground, scared to
        nibble at the rose's

last leaves?

The Promise

While I wait for you to come to bed
my eyes are drawn to my self, below me
tan as an oil lamp's shadow
my breasts so womanish I wonder
why I haven't seen this before, or I think
how like me to have always imagined them
as girls' breasts.
When my mother was the age I am now
I wasn't yet born,
almost no way to remember
I'm grown now
and the reflex of love keeps interrupting.
In bed now, your lips miss my mouth
kissing my chin.
Elaborate return,
solitary, untangled lie.
You beside me
your own dream of your own body
here
learning to sleep.

Mother-Prayer

When I hear a voice connected
so completely to her infant
my knees shake. Strange to live
so close to another and so outside yourself.
But I've done it for a year now and think
how my mother did this four times over.
We compare notes this way: when was
the last time we washed our hair or
paid attention to the stained shirt we're wearing?
A weird joy to be so mindless of ourselves.
Our babies.

When I was 17 my own words
were insult in my head. Smooth and stony
pills filled one palm, faucet water dashed
through the fingers of the other,
and trembling I dropped each pill
to the chrome cave
instead of into my waiting mouth.
Now some nights
cradling baby in the dark
I can feel that sweet fatigue.

When I stare into the mirror
I try to see the beauty there.
Instead I see just a face. I insist
tell me why you love me?
as though my husband could
return me to myself.
He can't budge me from this cliff's edge.
It's so dreamy on the other side.

Each time bread fell to the floor
my mother used to pick it up,
brush it quickly and say
Kiss it up to God before she placed it
firmly to our lips. And so I do,
I kiss this up.

Sometimes the Grief is Real

Sometimes the grief is real
and we go like soldiers to the ordeal
of happiness.

Sometimes the grief remembers us first
and we sit stunned in the sun's glare.

And sometimes grief gets abandoned,
forgotten,
and we are truly happy, we feel well fed

so that when it returns, raw and exhausting,
we don't want to make its bed, we don't want

to welcome it with new sheets or dinner. We want
to call for takeout. But it demands the full three-course
and dessert

and the attention accorded the dreadfully boring guest.

Hypothesis

What if it had been you who said
once you'd thought of killing yourself,
that more than once you'd thought
you hated your life but every way to end it
seemed too horrible, for me? What if
it had been you who cried past midnight,
each night holding your belly or your chest
as if your insides would fall out?
And what if it had been you
who held on to the possibility of dying
like a person who holds on to the memory
of an unworthy ex-love?
What if it were me who suggested,
arm's length away, that maybe a drug,
some small pill could keep you sane,
keep you near me, could make you love your life?
What if it were you who'd said
you'd find your own way back?
And once you had done it,
come back so whole, so entirely,
I could not recognize
ever having almost lost you?

Return

When I came back,
honeysuckled, repaired,
my long journey not over
but detained, remade
out of limbo and sleep and rot
I mistook the effort
for jubilation
and when I pressed hard
on the edges I'd torn
or mishandled while away so long
as a mime might press thin air
I saw how the audience might squirm
for there was nothing there at all
and I didn't realize then, or maybe
I was just unwilling to receive
the bad news that
I would have to return
again and again meeting
that phantom like a body within a body
that can never emerge, never be known,
that I would have to learn
over and over to retrieve myself
for the sake of others I've been
so bound to save.

Miró Sees The Devil

He smudges it between his blackened fingers,
smashes it into color,
swishes it between his crabapple cheeks,
carves it in wood,
wraps it in greasy meat wrappers
or fine Japanese papers,
nails it to plywood,
releases it like incense.
He says that once
he even drew it in the sand
knowing the sea would wash it away.
It is important, he says,
just to paint the devil, to paint it.
But he seems much too small for the devil
hunched over a collage on the floor,
his eyes so hard at their work
you can see the lines the muscles have formed
training his eyesight to focus
on the thing in front of him.
The concentration seems to grow in him,
not like a thought
or an idea or a joke,
but like a key you hold in your hand as a child,
small metal you don't let go of,
you hold it so long you forget it is there.
I think of Miró before he goes out for a walk,
or maybe just before dinner how
after a day with his oils and petrol
and his aluminum foils caked in paint
he must wash his hands and that
even after he scrubs the black

from the crevices, from under his nails,
from the hairs on his knuckles,
his hands will still be stained.
And I think how, in sleep, those hands
will clasp his wife, hold her in the darkness.

Lucky

It is not much to manage to be this old
somewhere in the midstream
with that thin strip of gray in my hair that I won't pull out.
When I lift your unwashed shirt to my face
the gesture feels as young as I was
the year we spent in my roach-infested room on 110th,
the year I would not let you move in though you moved in
clothes   books   smell of crumpled shirts   love
catching in my throat but you were not in
not fully there though we fell to the floor once after making love
and were amazed at how dirty the damned place was.

Sometime after I realized all the men I'd miss for you
I was mad for it, the life that would keep us cued for the familiar.
Our daughter now in love with us both
likes to make the bed with me, likes to roll in your clothes.
And I like to watch the two of you, her caught
in the exotically comfortable
and the ache of her screech to say catch me don't catch me,
already learning that sharp game of faith.

How We Met

In this story there is no alcohol and no marijuana,
just fine fingers, embrace of hands, a promise,

eye contact, perfect
understanding, silver rings.

I leave out splintered glass, broken coffee pot, can opener
as birthday gift, ugly hat I,

years later, give away.

In later stories I edit out: sex, rejection,
screams of *I hate you.* But nothing polite

replaces any of it. *We are what we are,*
not the original dim-witted man and woman

unaware of our potential to kill each other, but
dying all the time, we do love

and that's the only part of the story
I really do leave out.

Leaving the Countryside

The toads' preening cries down by the marsh,
the way they seemed loudest in the darkness,
mocking me as I tried to find Orion's Belt,
vanish tonight
as I flick on the headlights against a gray skyline,
watch the speedometer
for fear of state troopers hidden in bushes.
I can no longer remember
Green Mountains splaying the sky,
sounds of gravel knocking the edges of a narrow road.
I used to dream that one day
I'd possess a lie so edgy and dangerous,
so strong, it would pull me out of my life.
I return to city lawn that's just survived the spring drought,
an ancient lilac bare in May,
a fence too old to hold even the slightest leaning
of the small boy who'll call my daughter's name through
    crevices of light.
The house charges up
with energy that otherwise
might kill someone.
I must learn to feed on it in small doses,
like a delicacy,
or like water to parched lips,
or like the ordinary craved
by eccentrics and lunatics.

Homesick

I live in an old house in an old
New England town now,
not a toy town
as I used to think of all places not New York.
It's "real" here
but like life out of a box of dreams some days:
house   car   husband   child

And before them? I can't quite remember
what I did those days. Walked along city streets
stepping in to buy some groceries I didn't need.
A matchbox size of saffron. Infinitesimal.
Almonds in a tub. Olives glimmering in brine.

At times I feel abandoned
like a lover feels left no matter
how confident the other will return
or call next day. And in the pure spring
when one can't really remember the snow
or the cold that leaves the skin bitter and sensitive,
then, that false confidence
welling up in the throat—all the time knowing
it's just as easy to feel damned.

Once, my father played a song on the guitar
that was about the mountains.
I could not help envisioning Annie Oakley
in white boots with fringes
and this, like the smell of a roasted chestnut that no one eats,
always reminds me of winter.
Is that blind nostalgia?

Or love? Or the broad base of
come-from-ness
which isn't elegant, which only insists?

Our July

Dark summer, the house closed up
like a cellar, cool a production
of science—my father's idea—
one fan to pull cool air into the front of the house,
the other sucking hot air from the bedroom
into the world.
Summer not a swelter of sun rays, but a
darker fuming of tomatoes wrapped in newspaper
and basil roots dangling in juice glasses.
My parents' idea of shelter: something to do with
just enough and
beleaguering excess
until it tires as much
as July's damp souls. They tried to teach me
to give up to what's stronger,
to obey summer.
But instead I try to bully the heat
to reproduce the coolness
of those first summers, but I forget
to turn the blinds just so to scatter sun.
By 9 a.m. the apartment's tight with heat
and the whir of the fans, too small for these
prewar-building windows,
can't protect anything.

Song of the Third Generation

I learned to read in the dark,
in the car, wherever the light
moved, shifted. My mother believed
I would burn my eyes out.
Between the breath and the text
my birth and hers kept happening
in the late night
in the daily horoscopes
in the 4:30 Movie
and the huge picture books filled with Hollywood stars.
My Ava Gardner died my mother says.
My mother learned to read the text of a life
as her mother learned to translate *Il Progresso:*
by reading a bit of headline,
any little bit.
They could both predict disaster—my mother's
in American English: divorce, drug addiction
and insane asylums. Nonna's in Calabrian:
earthquakes earthquakes famine.
Somewhere between our mouths
and what we said is what we learned.
Somewhere in the old country
we breathed text
without knowing how to read.
I learned in the old way, too,
in a corner of the kitchen
watching my mother pour the batter
of flour and zucchini blossoms
into bright spattering oil,
or in the cool basement at the edge of the ironing board,
the lint speckling her dark sweater,

at her elbow as she whipped the cloth
beneath the needle of her industrial Singer.
No other record, no other text
exists but the buzzing and this way of learning
in the old way,
which is any way that we can.

Afternoons with My Mother

1.
She agrees to let me wash her hair
and style it. I'm amazed
at its strength and thickness.
As I towel the strands dry
she shuts her eyes, then opens them.
She is the baby in the crib.
I am the mother dangling charms before her eyes.
When our eyes meet
I could swallow her whole.
I kiss her forehead as if it were a charm
and I am the baby in the crib.

2.
When we watch television
she folds herself weak-stemmed
into the huge chair,
adjusts her short legs on the ottoman,
clasps her hands to her round belly.
She watches models circle
in sequin Mackay dresses
and marvels at the chiffon
like someone who's had nothing
all her life.
But I know better.
She's not the child
peering through the hole in the fence.
But she is, she is.

3.
The burn on my wrist, purplish,
dull-sheened,
the way the experts say
makeup should be—
the color of your skin,
but more so. She wears burns
up and down her arms, her legs,
wherever the oil spits
from the huge vats and pans
she uses to fry eggs at the nursing home.
Now when I look at my mark,
I don't think of my own carelessness
as I pulled the pan from the oven.
I think of her splotched arms,
the pain in her face when she says
"It's nothing." Liar.
It's something, dipping a burned wrist
in hot bath water.
It hurts for days.

4.
Bitter, bitter, the small lips,
the clenched hands.
Selfish and giving at once.
She stocks my refrigerator
with filet mignon, five-pound bags of onions,
lentil soup, tomatoes from her garden
so that I'm always eating at her table.
I'm hardly ever kind to her
yet she calls me kind, sees me bend and soften
as I pull more food from the fridge.

5.
She hears voices.
In dreams her mother appears
to warn her of deaths and illnesses,
her father holds her hand in the dark,
her older brother protects her on the street.
The dead don't frighten her.
One night, someone's birthday,
we fought.
My sister flung cottage cheese against the wall.
My mother swooned on the bed.
I was sure we'd killed her.
I ran to my father. She's dead. She's dead.
But she woke from the dead.
She is a friend of the dead.
She tells me how to prepare for her death,
how to divide her goods.
This smooth-skinned woman,
veins pumping nectars of life to her heart,
tries to make me imagine a life
where she is dead,
where she will be able to talk to me each night
in my dreams.

Visit and Departure

Why don't you say it?

Fight the bruise at your hip

or even this month's temper
flared at your ankles

the children know it

so stories go my brother and sister
who don't speak to each other
years making all of us prisoners even grief tires

or mother getting smaller in my arms

my dear my sweet who never could

and father well at least he's still

there with her whispering at the driveway

we pull away tumbling really in wrapped leather
air-conditioned rambling unit of us
and listen to agreed upon CDs like mice

ah we are happy and even somewhat rugged

early warnings are ignored
we believe

it will last because we've left

fed-upness to other couples and feed each other

the dear things and sweets
and make nothing of what can't be made better
and I learn it nothing stays and I stay for it

fantasy does not erase their wave

their gratitude for making me and me
grateful too

I do want to believe
a master plan claims us

down deep I hear the engine
which must hide its power and seamless
burn its oil and its fuel highways cramping its sylvan wheels

we return home and I am all muck in the sleep
of children and it's almost as though
nothing can stop us

Public Beach

She vowed not to collect the dimes pouring from her pocket
cursed the linoleum that caught each one
in a delicate swirl. After showering, she bound her hair
in a towel. Thinking ridiculous
even wildest nature could be rendered urban
unforgiving. Just whose luxury
was being sacrificed in the dank smells,
the clammy seats of the toilets, the moist sand
scraping her toes when she ought to be clean?
How could concrete take such a rough role,
bits of glass, dirt and stone?
Her daughter asked her once why it gleamed so.
And how could she decide which to expose first,
the blight of glittered lies her immigrant great grandparents
followed across the ocean like dogs on a trail,
or the stubborn little childhood stories
designed by some poet or fairy tale writer
to keep us from believing the real?

Because My Mother Taught Me to Sew

I feel oddly delectable today
imagining you walking with me,
holding hands with me as we still sometimes do.
Because you are still alive, and not
completely out of your mind!
Because you've been my best teacher. My mouth
and my ear. My worried brow
and my deep-singing headaches,
my ability to providence and decipher
texts and the curses that once filled
your sweet little throat. You are
my crooked sentence, my selected house,
my inability to keep anyone's secret.
In other cultures, the ghost of your own mother
would devour you, but here we recycle:
the ghost of her has been spit from your head
and you pile her insults
into the depths of my hands,
your storage, your cave, your pit,
your blessing house, the birthing room
of my fingers. I have lied to you.
I won't release those curses; you can't gain your freedom
through the embrace of your youngest daughter.
With joy we slip into tarantella, waltz,
switching places, but we return to our seats,
I do what you have taught me to do—gather up, stitch
more tightly, more tightly,
clever hems, unseeable seams, mending that mimics
the cloth's tight weave,
voices inseparable from fingers or thread.

II. Heavenly Bodies

Old Body

Sleeping Beauty's kingdom slept for longer
than we've been crying.
And didn't that story begin
with the pain of parents and an only child?
I am two dead babies so far. One more
and it will be almost my mother's story, too,
the same dumb well
that can't wail and carry on for its own sake.
Though in comparison, my life is charmed,
no 17-year-old American girl
translating bank warnings and eviction notices
into Italian for her parents.
Still, my babies follow me everywhere,
enter our dirty mixed up family with tender feet.

Joining so many other ghost babies at the table.
And we've set places for none of them.
I am sister, mother, daughter to them all.
Grief in the half shadows though I want to
get on with it.
No shelter.
The wild little unborns scoff.
Either way you'll join us, they seem to say.

When I turn my head in the car
I see one child, one car seat. The child is
smiling, dreaming of her birthday.
Perhaps the baby ghosts have lifted
their heavy business for a moment?
But instead of lightness
I feel only its strange borders

and no ending that can arrange this thing
for the moment when we awake.

At Six Months

I always imagine it happening
in the pink and maroon bathroom I grew up with
sun scattered through dirty Venetian blinds
but this was in the time before I was born:
There must have been a sign,
a wide dull pain at your back
rising like fever
and the gripping you thought were cramps
drawing you in from the farm's garden.
You must have grabbed your first-born,
found a safe-bounded place for his crawling
and then ventured to a room I can't imagine,
your small womb unaccommodating, gyrating,
the blood flooding the bowl until
what had shaped you for six months
dropped horribly into the water.
In all the times you'd told me this story
I had never thought about the pain.
But now my knees have trembled there, too,
the water of my own womb aching to burst,
and in the midst of the fear,
the doctor's speculum scraping my walls for signs of that labor,
I wanted to say, let it come
unready for this world
and like you
I would gather it from its fall,
offer its ten-inch body up to the doctors for inspection
as it entered unnamed
into the heavens.

Miscarriage

I saw the beating light that was your heart
pressing itself against the center of the dark screen.
I did not think of myself as your mother. I thought
of the flash of those glow necklaces
they sell at circuses and at Radio City Music Hall.
I tried not to think how they always burn out in a day.
I tried to believe in you.
But you burned out, for no reason at all.

There, you see how I have turned you into a you
when perhaps instead no head formed, or if a head, no eyes.
Perhaps no tail to swill you through
the tight sac. Perhaps you were no more
than a mistake of clashed cells
colliding, jerkily pressing.

Still, whoever, whatever you are,
I make a poem, literary trickery,
when you are nothing if not genuine
and so slow to go. A good trait,
not to abandon, not to wander off.

I wait for signs: cramps, blood, pain.
Nothing but quiet.
All flesh and hormones.
I'm asking you nicely,
abandon me now. Make my body mine again.
If you do, I promise, I will give you back
your lovely, your quiet, your harmless.

May 21, 1999: Tomorrow Would Be the Day of Your Birth

I haven't thought of you in many months,
the moon has turned full and waned and planets have emerged
that surprised even the astronomers. All since
you died. I don't believe in reincarnation as a rule.
But today I imagined that the house cat here
who pressed her side against my door to open it,
who meowed accusatorily at my stinginess, was you,
come back with your small heart the size of a pin.
I couldn't even touch that cat
so sure that in its other life I'd done it harm, betrayed it,
that my lungs had not filled full enough for two or that
the cells had not divided quickly to make room for you.
I walked, my stride slow and ponderous today.
I looked at everything
that was small and seemed to be running from me. The chipmunks,
the thrushes. The mountains
hushed me. I looked at all
that could not recede or be neglected. I felt the energy
that rises out of long grass and asphalt, that comes late
or early, that touches the trees and the dandelions,
those ugly sisters with their unkind leaves,
their worried thriving. I thought of all the things in this world
that are not sure or beautiful.

Children

there is no mother,
Only terrain . . .
—Charlotte Mandel

No, no, I am
        not done with you yet,
you two who fled
        or were expelled. The universe
holds you without
        my permission. I don't know
if you can walk yet. Or have
        words, or have seen earth's diseases,
its ravage, its surly mountains,
        its iced caverns, its desert lengths
where children are less alive than you two,
        or if you've felt
more than your brother and sister
        living on this side,
mothered, fathered with exacting attention
        they can't escape.
They don't know you, and I,
        only the limits of your power surface.
I called out to hold on, stay put
        but to you such pleas mean nothing.
Oceans are your home
        fog and cloud your natural blankets,
stars, dead stones shining
        to light your crazy journey
along with the others, the peopled fields
        collapsing out of my comprehension.
Children die, every day. You must
        know them, too, now. How do they fare?

What is your death like? Why do you
         come to me, resting and working
your limbs into such deep ties?
         There is no mother here,
only the surface of your father's skin
         on mine. Only desire
for this strange permission
         that comes from, what?
to husband the deep-seated eggs inside the flesh
         into a racing pool of live fish, sweet and delicious?
Did you take provisions when you left me? A sample
         of skin, a small tin of blood and milk?
Did you remember to forget the sloping brim
         of what held you, clasped you,
still young enough to swim freely
         but old enough to leave
your mark here? Did you
         leave anything behind,
a gift for your youngest brother?
         Is that why he emerged amazed and startled
and would not look at me, but at the light
         above my head? Did he mistake it
for the stories of the stars you left him?
         Is he glad he did not follow your fishy trail
to the middle ocean, clean, bright with the life
         of whale and shark?

The Bridge

I. Childbirth Class

She describes the pelvic bones as a bridge
through which the infant's head
maneuvers, forward, back,
head up, head down.
And she presses the demonstration doll,
plastic head, cloth-and-stuffing body,
around the airy womb, which is nothing,
air caught in plaster of Paris bone.
We hear the clicking of plastics.
The head down now, and under
the bridge. But now she says
imagine the infant beyond the bridge
its body still making its way
through our aching tunnels.

II. Miscarriages

It's the 59th Street Bridge
or the Queensboro Bridge depending
on where your loyalty lies.
But I see it from the middle of the East River.
I'm watching two babies, tiny,
looking at me once,
twice.
They're excellent swimmers.
I'm treading water.
I can't follow them.
I don't watch them all the way.

But they're heading
swiftly for the bridge;
it's night. Lights mark
its several arcs.
Without speaking
the babies say *don't worry*.

III. Third Trimester

Each evening I fall asleep
to memories of labor pain,
then wake, each morning,
to feel my taut-stretched belly,
the purple graves beneath my navel
like carvings in thick hide,
the ache between my thighs
announcing no birth yet
but the high-pitched hymn of waiting.

Bedrest

In a hurry for you, in fear of you.
Stuck here in waiting, yet
I pray for a slow July and more weight on the scale,
a purple August with a low rising under heavy hips.

What you must be wanting.

In my dreams you take such solid form
I hear adult speech out of your baby mouth—

But you are before:
You are speedy pulse
arms and legs palpating in blue liquid
your movement fish-like, smooth and swift
ruffling the waters
your tail whipping, the chug chug
of your rump against my rib
like the tide fussing between high and low.

And I'm waiting, small strength that is unbidden:
the miniature house on the miniature railroad track
blown down by my own breath's hurricane.

Like your strength turning under my thinning muscles.

Sinatra Days

She swings back and forth
her head half off the headrest.
I'm vaguely afraid she'll sweep it out too much.
I'm washing the dishes
to Glen Miller's Band marching into Poland
I'm waiting for the news to come on. *We've bombed Bosnia*
and *you know what happened in Israel?* But I don't yet
and the world flattens this way for more than myself
and the girl-baby swinging behind me.
I've got four more glasses to wash
and the pots and pans from last night. But I'm hoping
she'll sleep to the big band sounds,
to the wish wish of the sudsy water,
to the slow Sinatra segue, so that I can
"learn" something about the world.

For weeks my body seemed so
simply forgiven beneath hers
all of me there only to provide
the rising and falling
of rhythmical breath.
But after her 12-week-old birthday I knew
I couldn't stay with her.
We're both on our own now—
my body demands my return
and I want to want that return.

And my daughter, still safe there,
just missing
the railing of her Swingomatic
with each drowsy back and forth

that won't turn itself into deep morning sleep.
I guide her head out from under the swing,
keeping her body small and round
and placing her into the crib,
there there   no cry   I say,
trying to keep the fretting from my voice.
I'm convinced she'll sense it and raise those lids
no cry   she reaches her arms to me once more
no cry   and   *no cry*   and
no news of the world. So I turn off the radio,
my daily version of these slightest surrenders.

Early Song

I like to stand tall when I'm drunk
and feel the edge of that tottering
and know how possible it is to fall
or appear to be falling.
My daughter sleeps that sweet
smelly sleep of sweat,
the wide open mouth, the stretch of the jaw,
unlikely rose in the barnyard quilt.
Before sleep she's rationally given orders
to hold her carry her bring her directly to bed
though it's early, summer's 6 pm
outrageously bright but I obeyed drew the shades
and without dinner she sleeps now
and I sip beer on the porch and feel
the slight wind lifting the hair of my arms
and I know the delight of that letting go
tipsy mother writing
in the daylight.

Why It Is Difficult

That rough skein of hope rubs
the inside of my flesh this morning
and the wear of seasons
rides up these tired arms—
even the laundry seems complicated
or whether to wake our toddler
and insist on another day. She'll rise,
find a toy or some other way
to stay time. I'll stand impatient watching
the clock, her purposeful hands.
I can't predict if I'll fight it today,
that clammy feeling of too tired
as though there were three of us rather than two,
my mother, my daughter, me.
What was it that seemed easy or simple as a child?

I don't fight the fatigue. I am out of jokes and games
and rely on the stern get-dressed-in-five-minutes-or-no-Barney
but my mother's words return. I soften. I cajole.
There's no time for TV
but there is breakfast. It lands on the floor.
My daughter stares at the dry flakes of oatmeal
and I remember instantly
the way in which my mother would lose
the strength of the fight. We, too,
are always in love. More oatmeal
and then my half-smile strangling
that little girl into confusion. What will I allow?
When will I begin the howl and pound,
my fist on the floor beside her?
Only once in a blue moon. The moon

of my mother's hands around my small body.
Once she said she wished we kids "had never been born"
and my sister and I stopped dead
unbelieving. Now I carry my mother's endearments,
love, sweetie. I lead my daughter out to the car,
allow her the treat
of blowing the horn and waking the neighbors,
"Just one beep or you'll wake up the block!"
Another indulgence that betrays
the power of that first blow
and the years it will take before she learns
it's already done the waking, to learn
that there's a clangy, demonstrable unholiness
to everything we long for.

The Shield

It takes everything I've got
to hold this shield up at belly height—
not carved like Achilles'
with the city of marriage and festivals,
or that more compelling city
of war and terror and ambush—
filling the tin field of it instead
dust-filled engravings of children
refusing to finish their supper,
meager houses without garages or backyards,
no trees, playgrounds covered in chipped glass,
dark kitchens and dishes piling up in the sink.
I'm afraid if I drop this thing
my misery and everyone else's will multiply.
I have to remember to reverse the pictures,
gain my own perspective. I see some tiny rivers,
none wide enough to keep a village beating for long
and I see a large hand, graceful, cupped
and holding up its dismal world.
The children's tight-lipped I'm-about-to-wail expressions
make my jaw lock to look at them.
There are some sunrays but no shadows
so that perspective is both flat and deep,
uncanny in this way. I'm the woman
behind the shield, alarmed, barely able
to keep my arms straight with the weight and wondering
who this thing was meant to protect—
it covers the middle of me, the place where
another small body might lodge itself
next year or the year after,
the shield calling me

as it called Achilles back into the battle,
but I turn around, I scour the corners of the room to find
the sparkling helmet, the dangerous spear
Thetis brought down from the gods for her son—
nothing here but the shield, the scene, the glassy edges of
        that mirror,
and the hero/anti-hero, this woman here
eager for the battles to subside.

Bringing the Chrysanthemums Home

Nothing as brilliant as I'd supposed
in their brown paper buckets
faking their way as earthen pots
moisture gathering at their bottoms.
The flicker of red in their buds
mashed and broken to muddy wine.
Their yellow centers gnawing, really,
their ragged petals mini-teeth of resistance
that aren't even efforts at flowers.
The leaves weedy, and if not starving
thirsty for something other than this life.
Against the beige siding and the painted oak door
they're blood in the teeth of the papered lantern,
skeletons gnashing their knees in the brick.

Birthday

The day that divided the world,
split us in two. But what from what?
Eastern from Western? Tragic from Joyous? Careless from Careful?
All nonsense your daddy says. Just 5 o'clock news
which we mustn't permit. Still you cry.
Just a day, but your day.
And my day, birthing you in frenzy,
blessed moment of scorched hair and wild
peach smelling blood. That's you.
Years later, when your brother was born,
the rare smell we could not get enough of. Daddy watched
you and I breathe him, an elixir, a fantastic
frothy milkshake of birth. And I whispered *you, too,*
you, too. You believed me. So now,

you must believe me again. September 11th
is a set of words bent in rare sand,
some of it in the shape of a bird,
some in the shape of a missile
on a clear morning,
and some shaped to the curve of your hand
on your small belly in the middle of the night.

The Hill and the Girl

Stone at the top of the hill.
She barrels down. And again. Collecting
grass, dandelions. Watch her

roll away. Try not to think of rocks, upended
sticks. Her hair tousles.
Her arms tuck, her legs splay and dangle.
Returning to the top,

to me

we read the light engravings
on a stone, placed here for the death
of a girl, slim, wild? Racing time. Whatever

she lived she lived it here once, placed
hands on the ropes of the swings, threw pebbles
at playmates below. Did she live

long enough to dream of fire
ravaging her house, or to worry
her lack of speed at multiplication?

Even these await the girl who stands beside me,
who's old enough to read but not
to guess catastrophe.

We're quiet, uncomfortable with prayer.
Would she like such a stone? Would I
want a granite block near a place I loved?

But she should not be asked.
She's a girl, released, at last.

My Death

She didn't know if I'd be
dead or alive. When I came running to her bed
it proved nothing.
She wouldn't hold me but sobbed
sobbed as though her own grief
would comfort her. I couldn't
rescue her   *put the child in your arms*
She wouldn't tell me if the fear
was leaving her.
Later, her nose at my hip, swearing
she would think of it all day:
my eyes opening even in death
and when my eyes closed finally
my body scattered into a million little bodies.
In olden times, she says,
she knows people died
because there was no medicine.
Nights and nights before
I'd dreamed I'd lost her
in fields of high Nebraska grass,
then, somehow, forgotten her
in grave sleep, on dirty tiles
of the ladies room of some tired suburban mall,
its heavy door easing between us on its enormous spring.
Next morning she's laughing
it worked it worked, the dream-catcher worked
her footsteps down the stairs
heavy with speed.

Pumpkin Pie

Today I've made her pumpkin pie and given her a book
about a girl and a deer to celebrate
her tongue's first meeting with the communion host
which she's taken shyly from the priest
her hands cupping it so that her fingernails
flecked red and chipping show around the wafer.

She eats the secret flesh on the way back to the pew
laughing quietly and tells me when we've landed
how good it tastes. She sits halfway on her bench,
one sandaled foot tapping on the red vinyl kneeler,
the other dangling in the cool underneath air.

She winds her hands around
doing the sign of the cross a little backwards
a little upside down. She's six and a half.
When we go home, though it is spring,
I serve the favorite pie.

She eats a second piece because
she's forgotten whipped cream.
I've told her everything
before others get to her: that Catholic kids
like I was once have huge frosted cakes
and white frosted dresses and lots of money envelopes.

That night I hear her singing in that teasy way
        I take communion
            I take communion
But I don't scold her. Even Jesus teased his mother.

Mother and Daughter Home Sick

She sleeps on the couch, head like a mirror to me
perched on a pillow, warm breath, vision mouth,
neck a gamble of what it holds,
wrenching head one way, torso and hips another.
Small fingers warmed in frigid March
angle over the red wool blanket.
And just yesterday we held each other
and made excuses for terrible curses and screaming.
Innocence, forgetfulness, her drawn out breath
not a snore or a sigh yet something indelible,
maybe not blaming me but glimpsing in me something,
rage of the mother like a growth, a shoot of love
gone crazy in the not-yet spring light
where there should be no snow but is,
above the curbs and impatient iris greens.

III. Considering the Universe

Before Children

Danny Schwartz once told me
I'd make a good mother
because I'm kind, he said.
It took him three hours to make a deep-dish pizza
and I felt uncomfortable with his roommate,
a woman with thin lips who watched my mouth move as I ate.
On the way home I took Lexington Avenue
and in the 20's tried not to stare at the hookers and johns
dipping in and out of cars as the light was going and I thought,
I wish I could love a man like Danny.

This morning the red cardinal sang indifferent to me.
He was looking for someone else.
I have a daughter now and I think of that boy
who saw a goodness in me
that I try to retrieve, that I try to sustain
and then that ruby-red bird alone on the bough—
how harsh and gorgeous a cry
done for himself
and for the one he catches listening.

The Boy and the Stone

A boy picked up a stone and threw it,
it landed far out in the middle of the night,
it floated upward. It was not
responsible for anything. It did not cause
war to break out. It did not hurt anyone
or land on anyone's land. It wasn't part of the earth
but it didn't scorn earth either.

Soon the earth was filled with them,
these rocks that had floated long enough
and landed without as much as a thud.
The river mouths began to fill with them,
magic stones ordinary stones
flung with the purpose of strong tiny
fingers into the air into the night.

There is no accounting
for the nature of rocks. *So be it* they seem to say
though flung by the rancorous temper of a boy
they say *so be it* and neither sit nor sleep.
But the boy makes mistakes
and shifts his hand so that one stone
thrown outside of the dream
causes a million griefs.

Recovery Room

They'll take you away
if I ask them to. I want them to
put you in that mechanical swinging crib
in the room with the lights on all night.
I'm aching.
Go and don't go. You're screaming. I must sleep.

On the second day, we name you.
There are three of us
to welcome you. There are three of us
to take you home. We haven't called everyone
we should have. Only our mothers like your name.

The nurse comes in, stern, looks at me. *Your milk
hasn't come in yet. He's dehydrated. He has a fever.
You'll have to take that formula sample out of your bag.*
You feel as warm as you did yesterday.
I keep you on my breast all morning while the nurses
peek in to see if we are packed yet. They look at the clock.
They look at you. They are ready to report
your dehydration. They are ready to report
my inability to pack up three vases of fresh cut flowers
and an oddly parachuting hospital bag with things I have not used.
And you. I must pack you.

I'm sore. You're fevered. You're crying.
This is our leave-taking.
This is how we start again.

Travelogue

I feel that I should have come back from the dead
or returned instead
from the joy of another country
a well-worn travel
in which I would have witnessed
the demise of great dominions
and in their stead
common traffic, the city bus
cursed by long-waiting commuters,
gray-walled banks and post offices
once meant as the residencies of one
wealthy ruling family,
trees fairly surviving
the ravages of smoldered gunfire,
leaves torn off that way.
The rooms here now lined
with pastel blue cards,
best of luck. I hold luck in my hands,
a tiny boy baby
and have returned only
from the hospital back to
unopened newspapers,
poems I'd been editing, or rather,
much too tired and anxious to understand,
a book full of stickums with little notes
identifying their significance,
or worse no notes at all.
And flowers, stems compressed in straw baskets,
bowled glass
catching the mistake of sunlight from the front porch.

Practicing Peace

On Route 2 in Massachusetts
in Arlington or Belmont or Concord or
somewhere when we aren't paying attention
and before we make jokes
about dropping the kids off at the Concord jail
we see our first sign across the porch of a house set high
        over highway
practice peace. Hours later in Shelburne Falls
I see two more banners
one in the front yard white on black *pray for peace*
another spanning the front railings that just says *peace.*
Just before Greenfield in the backseat
our son cries pointing at his mouth
alerting us too late and yes
throws up all over himself
car seat and buckles and somehow
even the back of his pants. So that
the 9-mile trip between Greenfield and North Adams
takes two hours instead of less than one
and our daughter does what is asked of her
entertains him distracts him while we
wipe everything down with diaper wipes.
At the North Adams Holiday Inn
a lovely teenage waitress places
chicken dinner on a plate with a cover on a tray
slips a big fat steak knife between plate and chrome
while I roam through deserted aisles of Stop & Shop
for baby Tylenol and my husband returns to the room
with the tray with the sick son with the daughter still having
an oddly marvelous time
counting up hotel soaps and charting our next pool visit.

Practice peace pray practice
and now the boy sleeps, the girl tries to sleep
my husband and I move around in the half dark
having turned off the almost silent TV
and even though I still thought this morning
about reaching my 40s with way too much fat on my thighs
and not being famous I do forget
everything we fight over and I still want to practice
I still want to pray not only that I won't explode
but that I won't practice by pretending
to stay calm.

At the Rehearsal

I watch my girl, rows away,
strands of hair poking from the tight bun,
her lips moving, singing to herself,
or speaking to a friend I can't see from this angle,
waiting her turn to perform.
A rainstorm outside the cement hall
makes the other mothers announce as they enter,
so strong I had to pull over.
In this vacuum
the hum rises, women in our damp chinos
and our faux casual t-shirts,
daughters in black leotards, pink slippers,
muted boredom of the toddlers.
Sometimes I look around me I say to my friend and
she finishes, *this feels like someone else's life?*
and I nod yes because it's easier than explaining.
Rehearsal lights dim and brighten.
The boy on my lap watches girls dance
like cats or lit up fountains
as closely as he'd watched Sesame Street this morning,
a film of a girl on her way to school:
She stood slim and unmoving as her mother dropped
a sleeveless dress over her head, handed her a roll,
headed her off down the road
no shoes and the narrator announced, "Africa."
So I nod *yes someone else's life* but I think *no, this life is mine*
but also its explosion,
or its tiny alert with its piercing sound
or the silent emergence of it
the cruelty of its odd excess.

Grace

We can't quell it, reject it, despair of it.
We can't redirect it. It doesn't
fall down from a compassionate God
or derive out of a mad saint's prayer.
It is not salt it is not oil it is not ice it is not fire.
It's more than Jesus' face in the stained glass.
It's more than the glass.
It arrives even if you fear mountains,
sounds in the woods. It recognizes your disbelief.
And like a masochistic lover
it takes all of it. It has visited every nation
and the house of your brother, old boyfriends,
teachers who should have chosen another profession,
also the grieving, the happy, the brave. It's a seed,
it's a host. It's a terrible guide
that doesn't care if it sees in the dark
and doesn't care if you do. It's lighthearted
and it can hear you more than once. Did you
hear that? You have another chance
and another and another.

Considering the Universe

She asked could I tell
what's out there, what beyond
and how to travel it.
Would we die?
She can say
beyond the universe and *death*.
I crimp the quilt at her neck.
I say *god* and *trust*. But what
holds us? Stories, I think, but don't
utter. Safely put, my hands
move inside my lap.
She commits to live forever.
She can find out that way.
But all your friends, I think
and me
and the dark
my whole life
shortened, shapes of the already dead,
the soon-to-be dead, shapes
of nightlight-shadow on the wall.
I hear whispers, old women,
feel the breast of my mother
rising falling with mine
her *God* her *Jesus* her *Mary*
so easy to believe
she leaves prayers all over me
and her *G D* curses too
how lucky to know
how to pray so loud.

Buildings After the Ice Age

E. St. Vincent called it God's world
imagined buildings "million story high"
in her 1917 New York.
1942 Jenny, not yet my mother,
catches a needle in her eye
walks away from her machine without blinking,
tells no one, breathes shallow,
stations herself before the grimy mirror,
tips her index finger and waits
for the needle's middling roll, rolls it out.
Sinks back heavy in her work. Catches up
gets paid that day.
My husband's grandmother, Stella,
waits alone 30 stories up a midtown hotel in 1949,
rests on white sheets, paces windows to see Manhattan's grids
while her Midwestern man reports to his first day on the job.
1974 my best friend and I roam United Nations' broad plaza,
take our first panoramic photos,
river gleamy film behind us
each of us takes turns squeezing the shutter
squeezing our eyes against the dirty wind
and the same sun Vincent blessed.
1976 The Towers are hideous and just
keep climbing. My first boyfriend takes me
to Windows on the World. We spin but I'm
afraid to eat. Poverty and
my ugly brown suede boots.
Heady 1980s, everyone has money
and Norm and Liz and I write about it.
Someone's affair is fair gossip in the tunnel
from IRT to Winter Garden to leafing through

straight skirts on sale at Ann Taylor to the 52nd floor.
Silver gray suits and navy pumps select
each floor with cigarette grace.
On anxious days I wish that I could walk it.
5 p.m. from plush to the concourse.
I laugh at the Windows
on the World placard. I shop
at the Farmer's Market.
2001 New England autumn
first job where people call me professor
at a break in our three-hour class
I watch the Windows burst on a large-screen TV,
remember the man who sold me
bagel & cream cheese at the IRT.
I return to my classroom to tell them;
they send us home, lock university and museum.
I take the "T" home watch TV
wait for my daughter in her classroom,
pick up my son from day care, want
the ugly building I remember,
the people in it.

Lighting Out

Someone makes that move toward Bethlehem
(again)   succinct   undemanding
the star pointed toward the wrong king

      should we ask the questions
where are the children?
the tiny ancient footsteps?
      and
where did this story begin?

      this is the place where the ground trembled
shook us right off the rocks, the cliffs,
the precipice

this is the hand that touched itself in the dark wind
it is calm now   the hand   the wind
the lesson to follow stars so
                unadvised

we go walking

      my child's at the edge of the lake
learning to throw stones

how will she know how good she is
if I don't tell her. A million times one million

over the moon
      over the stars
follow this one

                              and that one

follow the good if you can believe it

          as I do

Saying Good Night In the Kitchen

My mother's forest body
is still my landscape
river veins   mountain legs   kitchen speed
at my ankles forest darkens
children press their rectangle foreheads
skin to skin   matching shapes
     waves of light
if spirits call my mother
she will leave me
rings on rounded knuckles
motion of age-sore hands
a sink full of greens, sandy and bright

About the Author

Julia Lisella is the author of *Love Song Hiroshima* (Finishing Line Press, 2004), a chapbook. She holds an M.A. in creative writing from New York University and a Ph.D. in English from Tufts University. She has received several community teaching grants through the Massachusetts Cultural Council and has held residencies at the MacDowell, Millay, and Dorset colonies for the arts. In addition, she is a scholar of modernist women's writing. Currently, she is assistant professor of American literature at Regis College in Weston, Massachusetts.

Printed in the United States
R3419300001B/R34193PG201715BVX1B/1-36/A